Introd

There are so many quilt blocks
ways to create totally different quilts. All a quilter has to do is
simply twist or turn them in their setting. With a good block
pattern and a quilter with an imagination, many unique quilts
can be made with a single block pattern. The eight quilts and
nine alternate diagrams in this book are only the beginning.
Our designers were asked to create blocks that could be
turned in their settings to create other fun quilts. I think they
met the challenge well and came up with some awesome
quilts. We only touched on some of the unique ways to place
these blocks, and my hope is that you will discover many
more. If you like the block pattern, don't be afraid to challenge
yourself to see just how many other ways you can set it.
We actually had many more options than we could add to
this book.

So next time you're looking for a fun quilt pattern, remember
to consider other ways to place these blocks. These patterns
are timeless, and I'm sure you will use them many times in
many ways if you allow yourself to play!

Enjoy!

Table of Contents

Twisted Fences

The combination of these two simple block units can be arranged in many different ways to create endless quilt designs.

Designed by Nancy Scott
Quilted by Masterpiece Quilting LLC

Skill Level
Confident Beginner

Finished Sizes
Quilt Size: 78" x 78"

Block Size: 12" x 12"

Number of Blocks: 36

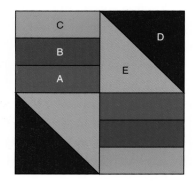

Twisted Fence
12" x 12" Finished Block
Make 36

Materials
- 1⅛ yards teal batik*
- 1⅜ yards pink batik*
- 1⅛ yards blue batik*
- 2¼ yards purple batik*
- 1⅔ yards light blue batik*
- Backing to size
- Batting to size*
- Thread
- Basic sewing tools and supplies

*Jewel Box fabric collection from Island Batik and Soft & Bright batting from The Warm Company used to make sample.

Project Notes
Read all instructions before beginning this project.

Stitch right sides together using a ¼" seam allowance unless otherwise specified.

Materials and cutting lists assume 40" of usable fabric width for yardage.

WOF – width of fabric

HST – half-square triangle ◻

QST – quarter-square triangle ⊠

Cutting

From teal batik cut:
- 72 (2½" x 6½") A rectangles

From pink batik cut:
- 36 (6⅞") E squares

From blue batik cut:
- 72 (2½" x 6½") B rectangles

From purple batik cut:
- 8 (3½" x WOF) F/G strips, stitch short ends to short ends, then subcut into:
    2 (3½" x 72½") F and 2 (3½" x 78½") G
    border strips
- 36 (6⅞") D squares

From light blue batik cut:
- 72 (2½" x 6½") C rectangles
- 8 (2¼" x WOF) binding strips

Inspiration

"The design challenge was my inspiration for this pattern. I started with some basic quilting units and then just played until I came up with a fun design with lots of variations." —Nancy Scott

Completing the Blocks

1. Stitch an A, B and C rectangle together as shown in Figure 1 to make a Rail Fence unit. Make 72.

Rail Fence Unit
Make 72

Figure 1

2. Draw a diagonal line on the wrong side of the E squares. Referring to Figure 2, pair an E and D square, right sides together. Stitch ¼" on each side of the drawn line. Cut on the line to make two D-E units. Press. Make 72.

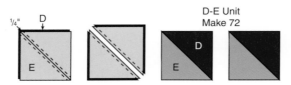

D-E Unit
Make 72

Figure 2

3. Refer to the block diagram and arrange two Rail Fence units and two D-E units in two rows. Stitch units into rows; stitch the rows together to make one block. Press. Make 36.

Completing the Quilt

Refer to the Assembly Diagram for steps 1 and 2.

1. Arrange blocks into six rows of six blocks each. Sew blocks into rows and sew rows together to complete the quilt center. Press.

2. Stitch one F strip to each side of the quilt center. Press, then stitch one G strip to the top and bottom. Press.

3. Layer, quilt as desired and bind referring to Quilting Basics. ●

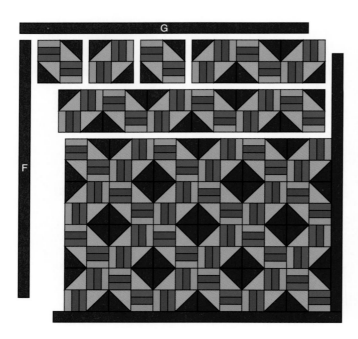

Twisted Fences
Assembly Diagram 78" x 78"

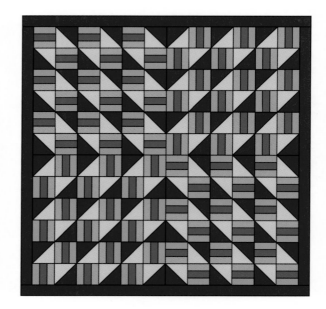

Twisted Fences
Alternate Layout
Placement Diagram 78" x 78"

Flights of Fancy

Showcase a fabric collection with Flying Geese units and then twist and turn the blocks to create many different looks. This pattern would work great for scrap fabrics as well.

Designed & Quilted by Julie Weaver

Skill Level
Confident Beginner

Finished Sizes
Quilt Size: 52" x 62"

Block Size: 10" x 10"

Number of Blocks: 20

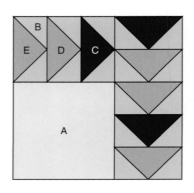

Flights of Fancy
10" x 10" Finished Block
Make 20

Materials
- ⅜ yard each of 3 different purples*
- ⅜ yard each of 3 different greens*
- ⅜ yard each of 2 different lilacs*
- ⅓ yard brown print*
- ¾ yard brown floral*
- ⅞ yard cream floral*
- 1 yard green print*
- 1⅔ yards cream tonal*
- Backing to size*
- Batting to size*
- Basic sewing tools and supplies

*Clover Meadow fabric collection from Moda Fabrics and Thermore batting from Hobbs used to make sample.

Designer's Tip

I chose to keep the colors of the flying geese sections the same throughout the quilt. The fabrics are different, but the colors are the same. Totally scrappy geese would look great also.

Project Notes

Read all instructions before beginning this project.

Stitch right sides together using a ¼" seam allowance unless otherwise specified.

Materials and cutting lists assume 40" of usable fabric width.

Draw a diagonal line from left to right across the back of all of the B squares.

WOF – width of fabric

HST – half-square triangle ◻

QST – quarter-square triangle ⊠

Cutting

From each purple cut:
- 20 (2½" x 4½") C rectangles (60 total)

From each green cut:
- 20 (2½" x 4½") D rectangles (60 total)

From each lilac cut:
- 20 (2½" x 4½") E rectangles (40 total)

Inspiration

"It's so much fun seeing how twisting and turning one quilt block can provide so many different looks. Flying geese units are one of the most versatile in the quilting world and I love them! This quilt could be entirely scrappy if someone wanted to use lots and lots of scraps." —Julie Weaver

From brown print cut:
- 5 (1½" x WOF) strips, stitch short ends to short ends, then subcut into:

    2 (1½" x 50½") F and 2 (1½" x 42½") G border strips

From brown floral cut:
- 6 (3½" x WOF) strips, stitch short ends to short ends, then subcut into:

    2 (3½" x 54½") L and 2 (3½" x 50½") M border strips

From cream floral cut:
- 20 (6½") A squares

From green print cut:
- 11 (1½" x WOF) strips, stitch short ends to short ends, then subcut into:

    2 (1½" x 52½") H, 2 (1½" x 44½") I, 2 (1½" x 60½") J and 2 (1½" x 52½") K border strips
- 6 (2½" x WOF) binding strips

From cream tonal cut:
- 320 (2½") B squares

Here's a Tip

Attention to pressing is important! Stitching the quilt together is so much easier when the blocks are nicely pressed.

Completing the Blocks

1. Draw a diagonal line corner to corner on the wrong side of all B squares as shown in Figure 1.

Figure 1

2. Position B right sides together on one end of C. Stitch on the drawn line. Trim seam allowance to ¼" and press, referring again to Figure 1.

3. Repeat with a second B on the opposite end of C to make a flying geese unit as shown in Figure 1.

4. Repeat steps 2 and 3 using B squares and C, D and E rectangles to make a total of 160 flying geese units.

5. Referring to Figure 2, lay out and stitch 20 three-unit sections and 20 five-unit sections using step 4 flying geese units.

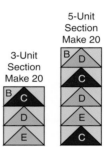

Figure 2

6. Stitch a three-unit section to the top of an A square as shown in Figure 3. Press.

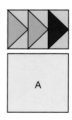

Figure 3

7. Stitch a 5-unit section to the right side of a step 6 unit as shown in Figure 4 to complete one block. Press.

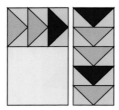

Figure 4

8. Repeat steps 6 and 7 to make a total of 20 blocks.

Completing the Quilt

Refer to the Assembly Diagram for steps 1–5.

1. Arrange blocks into five rows of four blocks each. Stitch blocks and then rows together. Press.

2. Stitch F strips to sides of quilt center. Press. Stitch G strips to top and bottom. Press.

3. Stitch H strips to sides of quilt. Press. Stitch I strips to top and bottom. Press.

4. Stitch L strips to sides of quilt. Press. Stitch M strips to top and bottom. Press.

5. Stitch J strips to sides of quilt. Press. Stitch K strips to top and bottom. Press.

6. Layer, quilt as desired and bind referring to Quilting Basics. ●

Flights of Fancy
Assembly Diagram 52" x 62"

Flights of Fancy
Alternate Layout
Placement Diagram 52" x 62"

Charleston Twist

This one simple block has many different looks when twisted and turned. You can create this quilt or its alternate option, or you can explore the many other ways this block can be placed.

Design by Lyn Brown
Quilted by Cathy O'Brien

Skill Level

Confident Beginner

Finished Sizes

Quilt Size: 57" x 77"

Block Size: 10" x 10"

Number of Blocks: 24

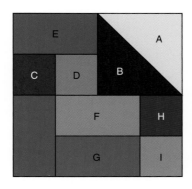

Twist
10" x 10" Finished Block
Make 24

Materials

- ¼ yard deep blue*
- ¼ yard bright green*
- ¼ yard dark green*
- ½ yard teal*
- ¼ yard light blue*
- ¾ yard turquoise*
- 1 yard dark blue*
- 2¼ yards light sky blue*
- Backing to size
- Batting to size
- Thread
- Basic sewing tools and supplies

Fabrics from Hoffman California-International used to make sample.

Here's a Tip

Value, the relative lightness or darkness of a color, is fun to play with here. Varying the value placement within the block will change the resulting secondary pattern. Try twisting the blocks in a different way (or add some sashing) for a totally different look.

Project Notes

Read all instructions before beginning this project.

Stitch right sides together using a ¼" seam allowance unless otherwise specified.

Material and cutting lists assume 40" of usable fabric width.

WOF – width of fabric

HST – half-square triangle ◻

QST – quarter-square triangle ⊠

Cutting

From deep blue cut:

- 24 (3") C squares

From bright green cut:

- 24 (3") D squares

From dark green cut:

- 24 (3") H squares

From teal cut:
- 24 (3" x 5½") F rectangles
- 24 (3") I squares

From light blue cut:
- 24 (3" x 5½") G rectangles

From turquoise cut:
- 48 (3" x 5½") E rectangles

From dark blue cut:
- 12 (5⅞") B squares
- 7 (2½" x WOF) binding strips

From light sky blue cut:
- 12 (5⅞") A squares
- 2 (9" x 57½") K borders on lengthwise grain
- 2 (9" x 60½") J borders on lengthwise grain

Completing the Blocks
1. Mark a diagonal line on all A squares.

2. Referring to Figure 1, with right sides together, stitch ¼" on either side of the diagonal line and cut on the line to make two A-B units; press . Make 24 A-B units.

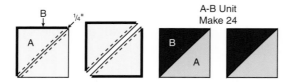

Figure 1

3. Stitch a C and D square together as shown in Figure 2. Press. Make 24 C-D units.

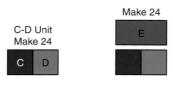

Figure 2   **Figure 3**

4. Stitch an E rectangle to the top of a C-D unit as shown in Figure 3. Press. Make 24 units.

5. Stitch an F and G rectangle together lengthwise as shown in Figure 4. Press Make 24 F-G units.

F-G Unit
Make 24

Figure 4

6. Stitch an I and H square together as shown in Figure 5. Press. Make 24 H-I units.

H-I Unit
Make 24

Figure 5

7. Referring to Figure 6, stitch an E rectangle to the left side of an F-G unit and an H-I unit to the right side. Press. Make 24 unit 1units.

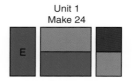

Unit 1
Make 24

Figure 6

8. Stitch a step 4 unit and an A-B unit together as shown in Figure 7, paying attention to orientation. Press. Make 24 unit 2 units.

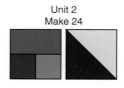

Unit 2
Make 24

Figure 7

9. Referring to the block drawing, stitch unit 1 and 2 from steps 7 and 8 together to make a Twist Block. Make 24 blocks.

Inspiration

"One visit to the beautiful low country of Charleston, S.C., conjured up vivid visions of cobblestones in seaside colors. Here, those historic cobbles mix with watery colors to bring the haunting charm of Charleston to this quilt. Vary the colors to make this quilt your own and to reflect your favorite place." —Lyn Brown

Completing the Quilt

Refer to the Assembly Diagram for steps 2 and 3.

1. Referring to Figure 8, position and stitch four blocks together, making a diamond in the center. Press. Repeat to make six block sections.

Block Section
Make 6

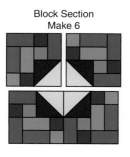

Figure 8

2. Stitch block sections into three rows of two sections each to complete the quilt center. Press.

3. Stitch J borders to sides and K borders to top and bottom of quilt.

4. Layer, quilt as desired and bind referring to Quilting Basics. ●

Here's a Tip

Constructing this quilt in four-block sections makes it easy to assemble—24 blocks "twist" to create just six sections!

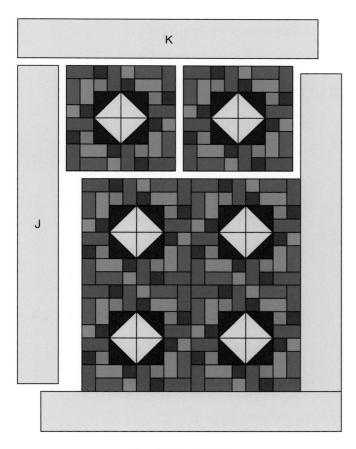

Charleston Twist
Assembly Diagram 57" x 77"

Butterfly Twist
Charleston Twist Alternate Layout
Placement Diagram 57" x 77"

Spin Wheels

This Y block has so many design possibilities. You can make this quilt as presented, or if you are looking for a table runner, you may want to use the alternate option.

Design by Cathey Laird of Cathey Marie Designs
Quilted by Karen Shields of Karen's Quilting Studio

Skill Level
Confident Beginner

Finished Sizes
Quilt Size: 56" x 68"

Block Size: 6" x 6"

Number of Blocks: 80

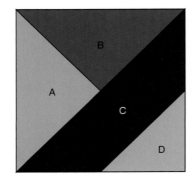

Y Block Variation
6" x 6" Finished Block
Make 80

Materials
- 1½ yards light*
- 1½ yards medium*
- 2⅓ yards dark*
- ¾ yard accent (teal)*
- Backing to size*
- Batting to size*
- Thread*
- Y Block Ruler™ by Cathey Marie Designs (optional)
- Basic sewing tools and supplies

*Stonehenge Gradations fabric collection from Northcott Fabric; Warm & Natural cotton batting from The Warm Company and 50wt thread from Aurifil used to make sample.

Project Notes
Read all instructions before beginning this project.

Stitch pieces together with ¼" seam allowance unless otherwise specified.

Material and cutting lists assume 40" of usable fabric width.

WOF – width of fabric

HST – half-square triangle ◺

QST – quarter-square triangle ⊠

Cutting

From light fabric cut:
- 20 (7½") A squares
- 6 (3" x WOF) strips, stitch short ends to short ends, then subcut into:
    2 (3" x 63½") G and 2 (3" x 56½") H border strips

From medium fabric cut:
- 20 (7½") B squares
- 6 (2" x WOF) strips, stitch short ends to short ends, then subcut into:
    2 (2" x 60½") E and 2 (2" x 51½") F border strips

From dark fabric cut:
- 40 (7") C squares then cut once diagonally ◺
- 7 (2½" x WOF) binding strips

From accent fabric cut:
- 80 (3¼") D squares

Inspiration

"I love thinking up new designs using the Y Block.
I never run out of ideas." —Cathey Laird

Completing the Blocks

1. Using Y Block Ruler, mark stitching lines on wrong side of all 20 B squares. If not using the Y Block Ruler, see the Alternate Technique sidebar.

2. Place marked B squares onto A squares, right sides together, and pin as shown in Figure 1.

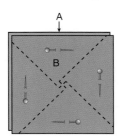

Figure 1

3. Sew on marked stitching lines in directions shown in ruler instructions. If square is wavy, press with dry iron before cutting. Repeat with all 20 A-B pairings.

4. Cut all A-B squares diagonally twice, corner to corner, as shown in Figure 2. Press seams toward B. This will yield 80 identical A-B units as shown in Figure 3.

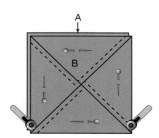

Figure 2

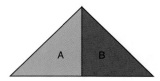

Figure 3

5. Referring to Figure 4, center and pin long sides of an A-B unit to a C triangle, right sides together, and sew a scant ¼" seam. Do not open or press yet. Pieces may not be exactly the same size, but no worries! The Y Block Ruler™ will resolve this.

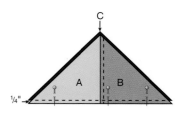

Figure 4

6. Using either the Y Block Ruler or your favorite method for squaring and trimming blocks, trim the step 5 units to 6½" square.

7. Snip seam allowance close to stitching line and press block open, flipping seam as shown in Figure 5.

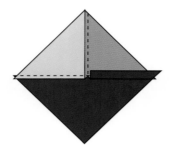

Figure 5

8. Repeat steps 5–7 to make 80 A-B-C units.

9. Draw a diagonal line, corner to corner, on the wrong side of all D squares.

10. Referring to Figure 6, place a marked D square on the C corner of an A-B-C unit. Sew on drawn line. Trim away excess fabric on corners leaving ¼" seam allowance. Press corner out as show on block drawing. Repeat to complete 80 blocks.

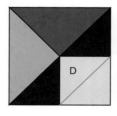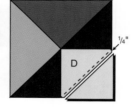

Figure 6

Completing the Quilt

Refer to the Assembly Diagram for steps 3 and 4.

1. Sew two blocks together as shown in Figure 7. Press toward B triangle. Make 40 block rows.

Make 40

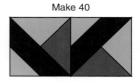

Figure 7

2. Arrange two block rows as shown in Figure 8. Join rows together and press. Make 20 block units.

Make 20

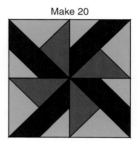

Figure 8

3. Lay out block units in five rows of four blocks and then sew into rows; press. Sew rows together; press.

4. Sew borders to quilt center in alphabetical order. Press all border seams outward.

5. Layer, quilt as desired and bind referring to Quilting Basics. ●

Here's a Tip

For precision piecing, place a pin vertically through fabrics at the exact points that need to match. Keeping the pin vertical, place pins slightly to the right and left. Remove vertical pin.

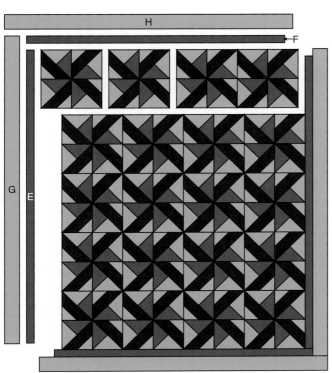

Spin Wheels
Assembly Diagram 56" x 68"

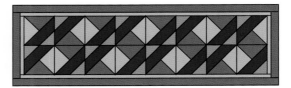

Spin Wheels
Alternate Layout
Placement Diagram 50" x 20"

I on U

By twisting the same block in different directions and using a variety of colors, you can make this quilt using endless combinations of block arrangements.

Designed & Quilted by Terri Butler of Mama Said Sew, LLC

Skill Level

Intermediate

Finished Sizes

Quilt Size: 62" x 79"

Block Size: 5¾" x 5¾"

Number of Blocks: 130

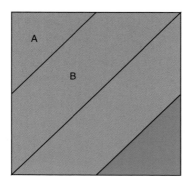

Diagonal Stripes
5¾" x 5¾" Finished Block
Make 130

Materials

- 1⅛ yards purple*
- 2⅛ yards dark orange*
- 1⅛ yards brown*
- 1⅝ yards blue*
- 1⅝ yards tan*
- ⅜ yard gold*
- Light box (optional)
- Add-a-Quarter tool for paper-piecing (optional)
- Backing to size
- Batting to size*
- Thread
- Template material
- Basic sewing tools and supplies

*Grunge by Basic Grey fabric collection from Moda Fabrics and Warm & White cotton batting from The Warm Company used to make sample.

Designer's Tip

It cannot be said enough to keep blocks organized! By working on one color combination at a time and labeling each block A–P, it will be much easier to keep your blocks organized. The blocks are rotated in different ways, so pay close attention to the quilt photo and Block Placement Diagram.

Project Notes

Read all instructions before beginning this project.

Stitch right sides together using a ¼" seam allowance unless otherwise specified.

Materials and cutting lists assume 40" of usable fabric width for yardage.

WOF – width of fabric

HST – half-square triangle ◻

QST – quarter-square triangle ⊠

Cutting

If using the template method to sew the blocks, prepare templates for trapezoid (B) and triangle (A). Refer to Figure 1 for cutting layouts and to the patterns for number to cut and color.

The designer used the foundation paper-piecing method to make her blocks. She rough-cut fabric pieces for paper-piecing using the same guidelines shown in Figure 1 and pattern information. A paper-piecing pattern has been provided. Refer to Paper Piecing on page 28 to use this method.

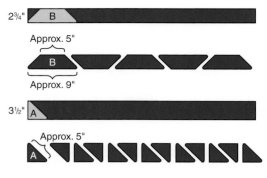

Figure 1

From dark orange cut:
- 4 (2½" x WOF) binding strips
- 4 (2¾" x WOF) D/F strips, stitch short ends to short ends, then subcut into:
    1 (2¾" x 75¼") D and 1 (2¾" x 62½") F border strip

From tan cut:
- 4 (2½" x WOF) binding strips
- 4 (2¾" x WOF) C/E strips, stitch short ends to short ends, then subcut into:
    1 (2¾" x 75¼") C strip and 1 (2¾" x 62½") E border strip

Completing the Blocks

1. If using template method, sew the appropriately colored A and B pieces together to make blocks A–P as indicated in Figure 2. The blocks should measure 6¼" unfinished. Make 130 blocks total. ***Note:*** *If paper-piecing blocks, refer to Paper Piecing instructions to make blocks A–P as shown in Figure 2.*

Completing the Quilt

1. Referring to the Block Placement Diagram, arrange blocks into 13 rows of 10 blocks each. Sew blocks into rows and sew rows together to complete the quilt center. Press.

2. Referring to the Assembly Diagram, stitch border strips on in alphabetical order. Press.

3. Layer, quilt as desired and bind referring to Quilting Basics and attaching the binding color to match the border strips. ●

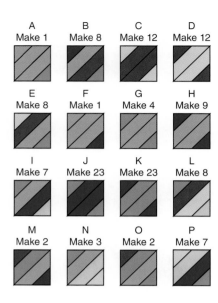

Figure 2

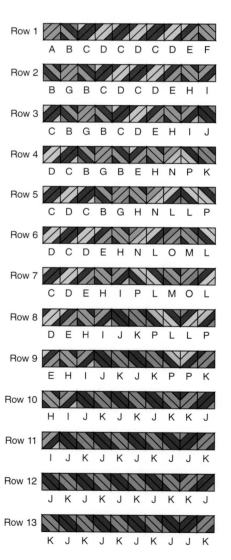

I on U
Block Placement Diagram

I on U
Assembly Diagram 62" x 79"

I on U
Alternate Layout #1
Placement Diagram 62" x 79"

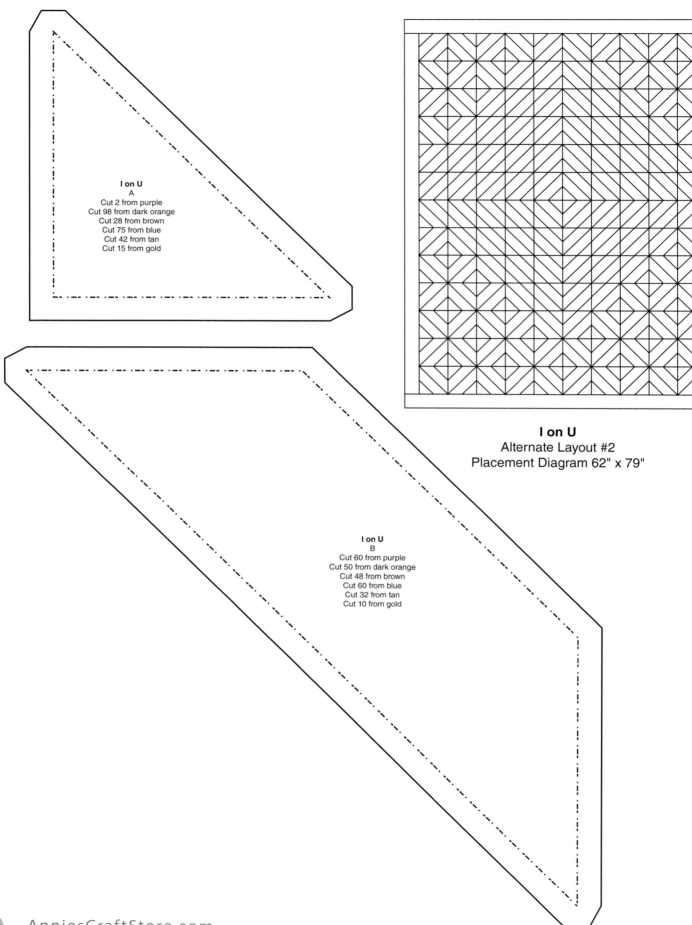

I on U
A
Cut 2 from purple
Cut 98 from dark orange
Cut 28 from brown
Cut 75 from blue
Cut 42 from tan
Cut 15 from gold

I on U
Alternate Layout #2
Placement Diagram 62" x 79"

I on U
B
Cut 60 from purple
Cut 50 from dark orange
Cut 48 from brown
Cut 60 from blue
Cut 32 from tan
Cut 10 from gold

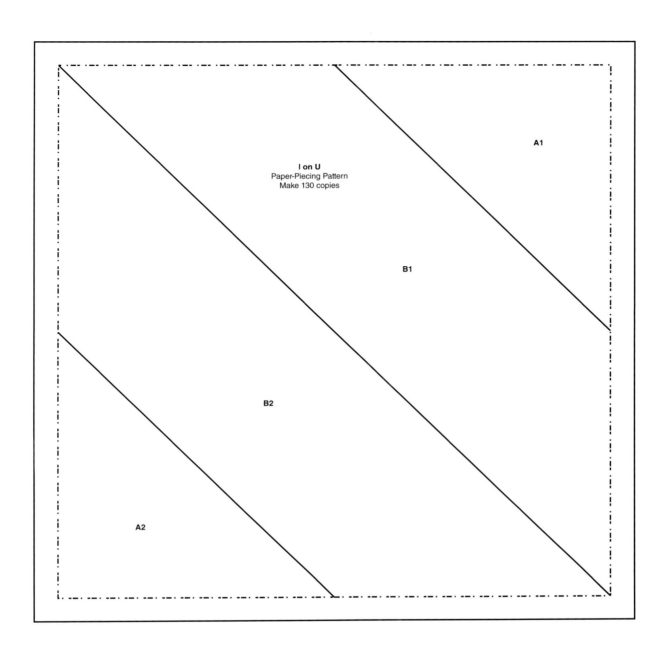

I on U
Paper-Piecing Pattern
Make 130 copies

A1

B1

B2

A2

Paper Piecing

One of the oldest quilting techniques, paper piecing allows a quilter to make blocks with odd-shaped and/or small pieces. The paper is carefully removed when the block is completed. The following instructions are for one type of paper-piecing technique; refer to a comprehensive quilting guide for other types of paper piecing.

1. Make same-size photocopies of the paper-piecing pattern given as directed on the pattern. There are several choices in regular papers as well as water-soluble papers that can be used, which are available at your local office-supply store, quilt shop or online.

2. Cut out the patterns leaving a margin around the outside bold lines as shown in Figure A. All patterns are reversed on the paper copies. Pattern color choices can be written in each numbered space on the marked side of each copy.

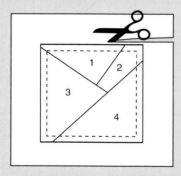

Figure A

3. When cutting fabric for paper piecing, the pieces do not have to be the exact size and shape of the area to be covered. Cut fabric pieces the general shape and ¼"–½" larger than the design area to be covered. This makes paper-piecing a good way to use up scraps.

4. With the printed side of the pattern facing you, fold along each line of the pattern as shown in Figure B, creasing the stitching lines. This will help in trimming the fabric seam allowances and in removing the paper when you are finished stitching.

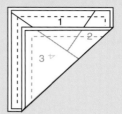

Figure B

5. Turn the paper pattern over with the unmarked side facing you and position fabric indicated on pattern right side up over the space marked 1. Hold the paper up to a window or over a light box to make sure that the fabric overlaps all sides of space 1 at least ¼" from the printed side of the pattern as shown in Figure C. Pin to hold fabric in place. **Note:** You can also use a light touch of glue stick. Too much glue will make the paper difficult to remove.

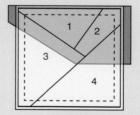

Figure C

6. Turn the paper over with the right side of the paper facing you, and fold the paper along the lines between sections 1 and 2. Trim fabric to about ¼" from the folded edge as shown in Figure D.

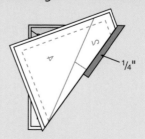

Figure D

7. *Place the second fabric indicated right sides together with first piece. Fabric edges should be even along line between spaces 1 and 2 as shown in Figure E. Fold fabric over and check to see if second fabric piece will cover space 2.*

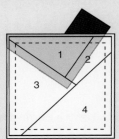

Figure E

8. *With the right side of the paper facing you, hold fabric pieces together and stitch along the line between spaces 1 and 2 as shown in Figure F using a very small stitch length (18–20 stitches per inch).* **Note:** Using a smaller stitch length will make removing paper easier because it creates a tear line at the seam. *Always begin and end seam by sewing two to three stitches beyond the line. You do not need to backstitch. When the beginning of the seam is at the edge of the pattern, start sewing at the solid outside line of the pattern.*

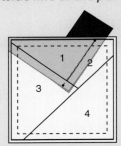

Figure F

9. *Turn the pattern over, flip the second fabric back and finger-press as shown in Figure G.*

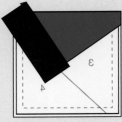

Figure G

10. *Continue trimming and sewing pieces in numerical order until the pattern is completely covered. Make sure pieces along the outer edge extend past the solid line to allow for a ¼" seam allowance as shown in Figure H.*

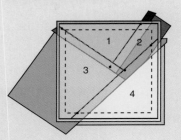

Figure H

11. *When the entire block is sewn, press the block and trim all excess fabric from the block along the outside-edge solid line of paper pattern as shown in Figure I.*

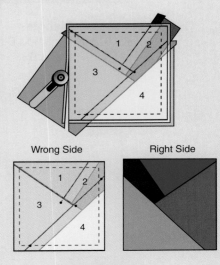

Wrong Side   Right Side

Figure I

12. *After stitching blocks together, carefully remove the backing paper from completed blocks and press seams. Or, staystitch ⅛" from the outer edge of the completed block. Carefully remove backing paper and press seams. Then complete quilt top assembly.*

Beach Glass

This easy one-block design invites you to twist and turn until you have your own beach treasure.

Design by Robin Koehler of Nestlings by Robin
Quilted by Toddy Sumsky

Skill Level
Confident Beginner

Finished Sizes
Quilt Size: 56" x 72"

Block Size: 8" x 8"

Number of Blocks: 63

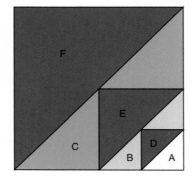

Triangles
8" x 8" Finished Block
Make 63

Materials
- ⅜ yard white*
- ⅝ yard light aqua*
- 1⅓ yards medium aqua*
- 3⅝ yards dark aqua*
- Backing to size
- Batting to size
- Thread
- Quilter's Rule™ Quick Quarter II Triangle Square Piecing Ruler 12" x ½" (optional)
- Mary Ellen's Best Press (optional)
- Basic sewing tools and supplies

Sea from Space batik collection from Connecting Threads; "Sally by the Seashore" quilting design used to make sample.

Project Notes
Read all instructions before beginning this project.

Stitch pieces together with ¼" seam allowance unless otherwise specified.

Material and cutting lists assume 40" of usable fabric width.

WOF – width of fabric

HST – half-square triangle ◩

QST – quarter-square triangle ⊠

Cutting

From white cut:
- 32 (3") A squares

From light aqua cut:
- 63 (2⅞") B squares then cut once diagonally �

From medium aqua cut:
- 63 (4⅞") C squares then cut once diagonally ◩

From dark aqua cut:
- 32 (3") D squares
- 32 (4⅞") E squares then cut once diagonally (discard 1 HST) ◩
- 32 (8⅞") F squares then cut once diagonally (discard 1 HST) ◩
- 7 (2½" x WOF) binding strips

Inspiration

"I've lived near many beaches and love to watch the sun glint off the moving water. The triangular edges are reminiscent of that shimmer effect and remind me of the many beach walks taken with my family. Of course, the bigger inspiration is how many different designs I can I create from rearranging these blocks."
—Robin Koehler

Completing the Blocks

1. Draw a diagonal line, corner to corner, on the wrong side of A squares. If desired, draw sewing lines ¼" either side of the diagonal line using Quick Quarter II Triangle Square Piecing Ruler.

2. Referring to Figure 1, place one each A and D square right sides together. Stitch ¼" on each side of the drawn line. Cut apart on drawn line, open and press seam toward D. Trim unit to 2½" with seam line centered.

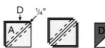

Figure 1

3. Repeat step 2 with remaining A and D squares to make 64 A-D units. Discard one unit.

Here's a Tip

When working with bias edges, spray sewn seams with Mary Ellen's Best Press or starch before pressing open to stabilize bias edges. Always handle bias edges carefully to prevent distortion.

4. Sew a B triangle on the top and left side of an A-D unit, aligning outer edges as shown in Figure 2 and sewing in the direction of the arrows. Press toward B. Make 63 corner units.

Figure 2   **Figure 3**

5. Fold an E triangle in half and gently finger-press to crease center as shown in Figure 3.

6. Place an E triangle right sides together with a corner unit from step 4, aligning fold with center seam of corner unit. Pin seam at the center and each end as shown in Figure 4.

Figure 4

7. Sew scant ¼" seam with corner unit on top so seams are visible as shown in Figure 5, to help make your points more accurate. Open unit and press toward E. Make 63 units.

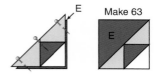

Figure 5

8. Referring to step 4, sew a C triangle along the top and left side of a unit from step 7 as shown in Figure 6. Make 63 half units.

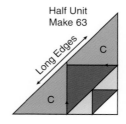

Figure 6

9. Referring to step 5, fold an F triangle in half and gently finger-press to crease center.

10. Sew an F triangle to a half unit from step 8, referring to steps 6 and 7. Press seam toward F to complete one block.

11. Repeat steps 9 and 10 to make 63 blocks.

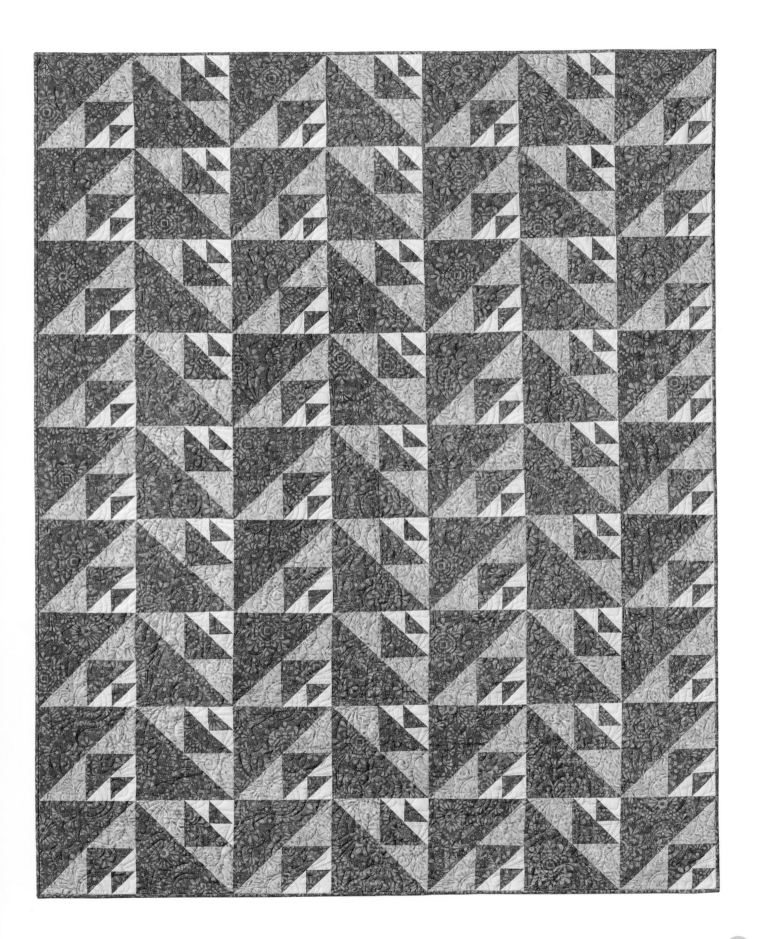

Completing the Quilt

1. Sew nine blocks together in a vertical row, placing the A-D unit in the lower right corner as shown in Figure 7. Press all seams the same direction. Make four rows.

2. Sew nine blocks together in a vertical row, placing the A-D unit in the upper right corner position as shown in Figure 8. Press all seams in the opposite direction of step 1 rows. Make three rows.

3. Referring to the Assembly Diagram, arrange and sew the vertical rows together. Press well.

4. Layer, quilt as desired and bind referring to Quilting Basics. ●

Here's a Tip

Don't forget to label and date your work!

Vertical Row 1
Make 4

Vertical Row 2
Make 3

Figure 7

Figure 8

Beach Glass
Assembly Diagram 56" x 72"

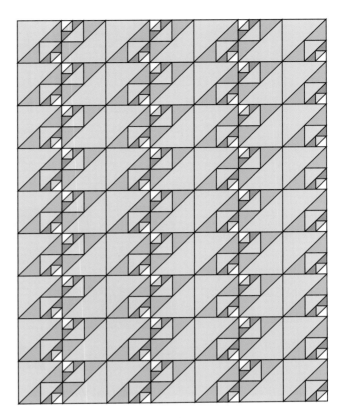

Beach Glass
Alternate Layout
Placement Diagram 56" x 72"

The Courtyard

Use this fun twisted block to make a table runner or take it one step further and add more blocks to make a lap quilt. It's a great block to twist and turn!

Designed & Quilted by Julie Weaver

Skill Level
Confident Beginner

Finished Sizes
Runner Size: 56" x 18"

Block Size: 6" x 6"

Number of Blocks: 16

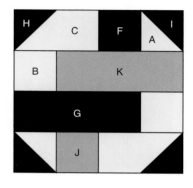

Snowball Variation
6" x 6" Finished Block
Make 16

Materials
- ¾ yard cream print*
- ½ yard black print #1*
- ⅓ yard black print #2*
- ⅓ yard gray print*
- ⅔ yard black floral*
- Backing to size*
- Batting to size*
- Thread
- Basic sewing tools and supplies

*Stiletto fabric collection from Moda Fabrics and Warm & Natural cotton batting from The Warm Company used to make sample.

Project Notes
Read all instructions before beginning this project.

Stitch right sides together using a ¼" seam allowance unless otherwise specified.

Materials and cutting lists assume 40" of usable fabric width for yardage.

WOF – width of fabric

HST – half-square triangle ◨

QST – quarter-square triangle ⊠

Cutting

From cream print cut:
- 16 (2½") A squares
- 32 (2") B squares
- 32 (2" x 3½") C rectangles
- 4 (1" x WOF) strips, stitch short ends to short ends, then subcut into:
    2 (1" x 50½") D and 2 (1" x 15½") E border strips

From black print #1 cut:
- 16 (2") F squares
- 16 (2" x 5") G rectangles
- 4 (1½" x WOF) strips, stitch short ends to short ends, then subcut into:
    2 (1½" x 48½") L and 2 (1½" x 14½") M border strips

From black print #2 cut:
- 32 (2") H squares
- 16 (2½") I squares

From gray print cut:
- 16 (2") J squares
- 16 (2" x 5") K rectangles

From black floral cut:
- 3 (2" x WOF) strips, stitch short ends to short ends, then subcut into:
    - 2 (2" x 51½") N and 2 (2" x 18½") O border strips
- 4 (2½" x WOF) binding strips

Completing the Blocks

1. Draw a diagonal line, corner to corner, on the wrong side of all A and H squares.

2. Referring to Figure 1, place A, right sides together, on I. Stitch ¼" on each side of the drawn line. Cut apart on the drawn line, open and press seam toward I. Trim unit to 2" with seam line centered.

Figure 1

3. Repeat step 2 with remaining A and I squares to make a total of 32 A-I units.

4. Place H, right sides together, on the left end of C as shown in Figure 2. Stitch on the drawn line. Trim ¼" from the drawn line, open and press seam toward H.

Figure 2

5. Repeat step 4 with remaining H squares and C rectangles to make a total of 32 C-H units.

6. Lay out pieces and units for one block as shown in block drawing. Sew units/pieces into rows and join rows to complete one block. Make 16 blocks.

Completing the Runner
Refer to the Assembly Diagram for steps 1–4.

1. Arrange blocks in eight vertical rows of two blocks each. When you are satisfied with placement, sew blocks together in vertical rows. Press. Sew vertical rows together. Press.

Designer's Tip

There are quite a few seams that need to be matched when sewing the blocks together for this runner. I thought it would be easier to have to deal with the seams on two blocks at a time, which is why I sewed the blocks together vertically. I know it helped me doing it this way! Pressing is also very important when there are lots of seams. Attention to pressing during construction will make the blocks go together that much easier.

The Courtyard
Assembly Diagram 56" x 18"

2. Stitch one L border to the top and bottom of the quilt center. Press. Stitch one M border to each side. Press.

3. Stitch one D border to the top and bottom of the quilt center. Press. Stitch one E border to each side. Press.

4. Stitch one N border to the top and bottom of the quilt center. Press. Stitch one O border to each side. Press.

5. Layer, quilt as desired and bind referring to Quilting Basics. ●

The Courtyard
Alternate Layout
Placement Diagram 24" x 60"

Square Dance

This large block is much simpler than it looks. Break it down into smaller units, twist and turn them until you like how they look together, and then stitch them together to make a fun quilt that will leave you friends and family wondering how it was assembled.

Designed & Quilted by Kerry Foster

Skill Level

Intermediate

Finished Sizes

Quilt Size: 54" x 72"

Block Size: 18" x 18"

Number of Blocks: 12

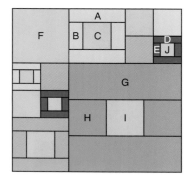

Square Dance
18" x 18" Finished Block
Make 12

Materials

- ½ yard each yellow, aqua and dark blue solids
- ½ yard each: 2 each orange, light green and red, and 1 each green and yellow prints
- ⅝ yard teal print
- ½ yard geometric print
- Backing to size
- Batting to size
- Basic sewing tools and supplies

Project Notes

Read all instructions before beginning this project.

Stitch right sides together using a ¼" seam allowance unless otherwise specified.

Materials and cutting lists assume 40" of usable fabric width.

This quilt is made from 12 (18") blocks all constructed the same but using different combinations of fabric.

WOF – width of fabric

HST – half-square triangle ◩

QST – quarter-square triangle ⊠

Cutting

From geometric print cut:

- 7 (2¼" x WOF) binding strips

Here's a Tip

This quilt uses 12 different fabrics in a plethora of colors and prints to make 12 blocks.

You may choose unusual prints to showcase and/or fussy-cut for the square pieces. Just remember to also include some coordinating solids to give your eyes a place to rest.

Inspiration

"This is the second time I've made this quilt, which isn't something I do very often. I wanted a quick and easy design that I could make up in a long weekend and still look complicated whilst only using regular straight piecing with no triangles! I began by taking a square and dividing it up several times before it became the block." —Kerry Foster

For all other fabrics:

- Refer to the Cutting Chart provided to cut the correct number and size of pieces from the correct fabric. Cut all fabrics before beginning construction.

- To keep pieces organized, label 12 large plastic zipper bags 1–12. As you cut pieces from each fabric, place them into the appropriate bag according to the Block Chart.

CUTTING CHART

Colors	A 2" x 6½"	B 2" x 3½"	C 3½" x 3½"	D 1¼" x 3½"	E 1¼" x 2"	F 6½" x 6½"	G 4¼" x 12½"	H 5" x 5"	I 5" x 5"	J 2" x 2"
Teal print	16	16	15	2	2					
Orange print 1	2	2	1	2	2		4	4		
Yellow solid			12						3	9
Light green print 1	4	4	6	4	4	3	2	2	1	3
Orange print 2	16	16	8	16	16	1				
Green print			12						3	9
Aqua solid	6	6	10	4	4	3			1	3
Red print 1			4			1	4	4	1	3
Yellow print	4	4	4			1	4	4		
Dark blue solid			12						3	9
Red print 2				44	44	3	2	2		
Light green print 2							8	8		

BLOCK CHART

Block	Teal print	Orange print 1	Yellow solid	Light green print 1	Orange print 2	Green print	Aqua solid	Red print 1	Yellow print	Dark blue solid	Red print 2	Light green print 2
1	2 each A, B, C	2 each G, H	1 each F, I 4 C & 3 J	2 each A, B, D, E & 1 C							4 each D, E	
2					2 each A, B, D, E & 1 C	1 each F, I 4 C & 3 J	2 each A, B, C	2 each G, H			4 each D, E	
3	2 each A, B, C			2 each A, B, D, E & 1 C					2 each G, H	1 each F, I 4 C & 3 J	4 each D, E	
4	2 each A, B, C			1 each F, I 4 C & 3 J	2 each A, B, D, E & 1 C						4 each D, E	2 each G, H
5	2 each A, B, C		1 each F, I 4 C & 3 J		2 each A, B, D, E & 1 C		4 each D, E				2 each G, H	
6	2 each A, B, C				2 each A, B, D, E & 1 C		1 each F, I 4 C & 3 J				4 each D, E	2 each G, H
7	2 each A, B, D, E & 1 C						2 each A, B, C	1 each F, I 4 C & 3 J	2 each G, H		4 each D, E	
8					2 each A, B, D, E & 1 C			2 each A, B, C	1 each F, I 4 C & 3 J		4 each D, E	2 each G, H
9		2 each G, H			2 each A, B, D, E & 1 C	1 each F, I 4 C & 3 J	2 each A, B, C				2 each G, H	
10	2 each A, B, C				2 each A, B, D, E & 1 C					1 each F, I 4 C & 3 J	4 each D, E	2 each G, H
11			2 each G, H		2 each A, B, D, E & 1 C	1 each F, I 4 C & 3 J				2 each A, B, C	4 each D, E	
12	2 each A, B, C	2 each A, B, D, E & 1 C	1 each F, I 4 C & 3 J						2 each G, H		4 each D, E	

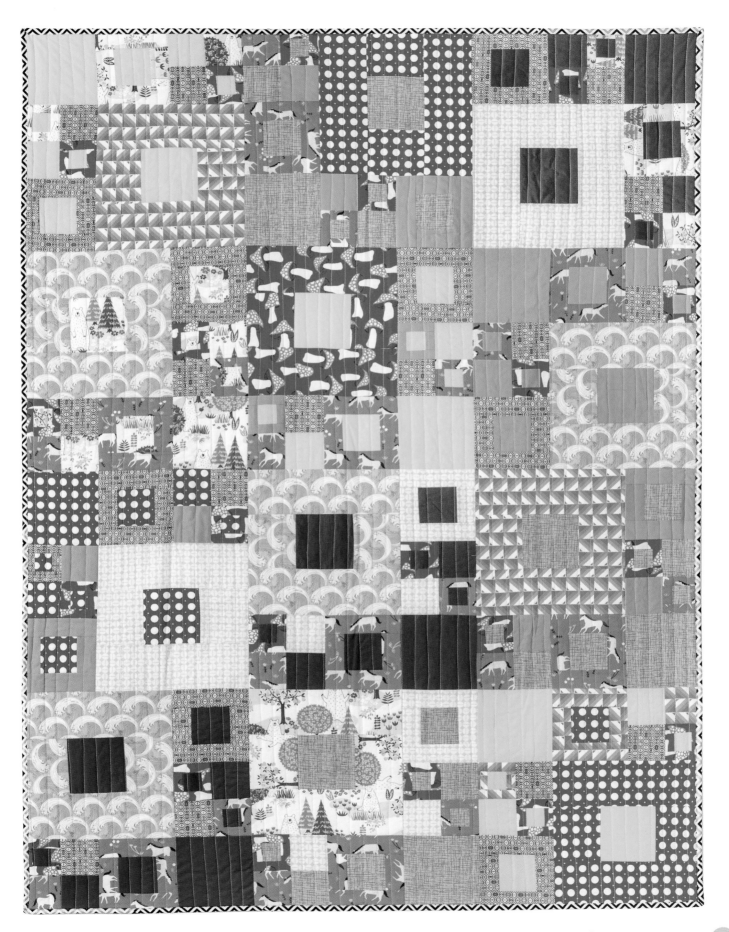

Completing the Blocks

Colors of pieces will vary depending on block and placement within block. Refer to the Assembly Diagram and Block Chart as needed.

1. For one block, make two A-B-C units, three D-E-J units and one G-H-I unit as shown in Figure 1. Press.

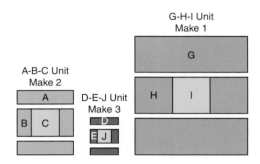

Figure 1

2. Stitch together three C squares and one D-E-J unit as shown in Figure 2 to make unit 1. Press.

Figure 2

3. Stitch two each C squares and D-E-J units together as shown in Figure 3 to make unit 2. Press.
Note: *The bottom left C square should be the same color as the F square cut for the block you are stitching.*

Figure 3

4. Stitch an F square, unit 2 and an A-B-C unit together referring to Figure 4 to make side section 1. Press.

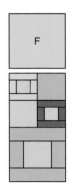

Figure 4

5. Stitch the remaining A-B-C unit and unit 1 together as shown in Figure 5. Press.

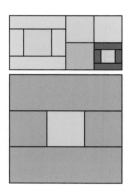

Figure 5

6. Stitch the G-H-I unit together with the step 5 unit referring again to Figure 5 to make side section 2.

7. Referring to the block diagram, stitch side sections 1 and 2 together to complete one block. Press.

8. Repeat steps 1–7 using fabrics as sorted to complete 12 blocks.

Completing the Quilt

1. Referring to the Assembly Diagram, stitch blocks together in four rows of three blocks each. Press. *Note: Each block is rotated so that the F square is positioned in a different corner row to row.*

2. Layer, quilt as desired and bind referring to Quilting Basics. ●

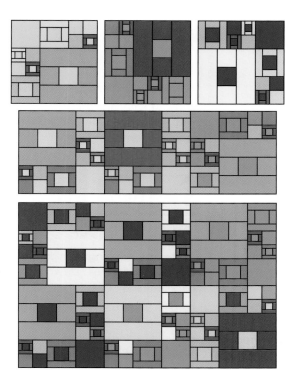

Square Dance
Assembly Diagram 54" x 72"

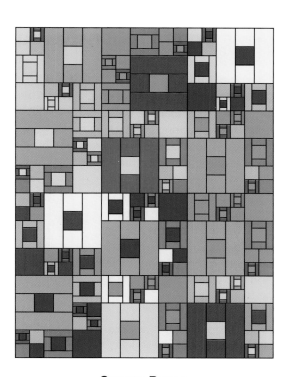

Square Dance
Alternate Layout
Placement Diagram 54" x 72"

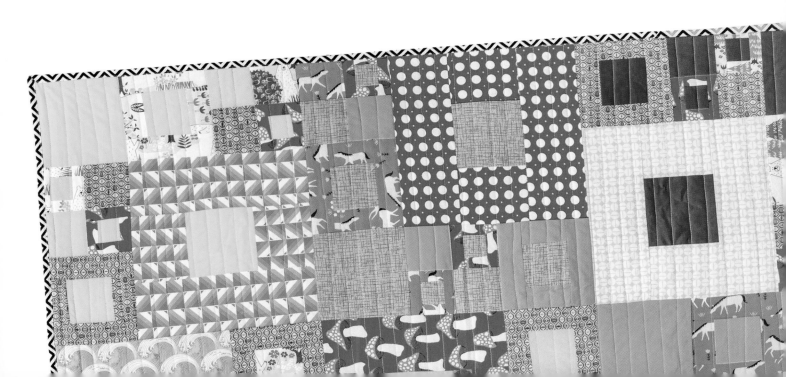

Quilting Basics

The following is a reference guide. For more information, consult a comprehensive quilting book.

Quilt Backing & Batting

We suggest that you cut your backing and batting 8" larger than the finished quilt-top size. If preparing the backing from standard-width fabrics, remove the selvages and sew two or three lengths together; press seams open. If using 108"-wide fabric, trim to size on the straight grain of the fabric.

Prepare batting the same size as your backing. You can purchase prepackaged sizes or battings by the yard and trim to size.

Quilting

1. Press quilt top on both sides and trim all loose threads.
2. Make a quilt sandwich by layering the backing right side down, batting and quilt top centered right side up on flat surface and smooth out. Pin or baste layers together to hold.
3. Mark quilting design on quilt top and quilt as desired by hand or machine. **Note:** *If you are sending your quilt to a professional quilter, contact them for specifics about preparing your quilt for quilting.*
4. When quilting is complete, remove pins or basting. Trim batting and backing edges even with raw edges of quilt top.

Binding the Quilt

1. Join binding strips on short ends with diagonal seams to make one long strip; trim seams to ¼" and press seams open (Figure A).

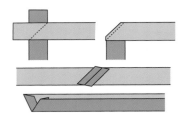

Figure A

2. Fold 1" of one short end to wrong side and press. Fold the binding strip in half with wrong sides together along length, again referring to Figure A; press.
3. Starting about 3" from the folded short end, sew binding to quilt top edges, matching raw edges and using a ¼" seam. Stop stitching ¼" from corner and backstitch (Figure B).

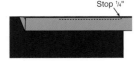

Stop ¼"

Figure B

4. Fold binding up at a 45-degree angle to seam and then down even with quilt edges, forming a pleat at corner, referring to Figure C.

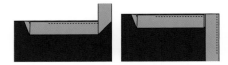

Figure C

5. Resume stitching from corner edge as shown in Figure C, down quilt side, backstitching ¼" from next corner. Repeat, mitering all corners, stitching to within 3" of starting point.
6. Trim binding end long enough to tuck inside starting end and complete stitching (Figure D).

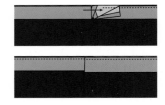

Figure D

7. Fold binding to quilt back and stitch in place by hand or machine to complete your quilt.

Quilting Skill Levels

- **Beginner:** A quilter who has been introduced to the basics of cutting, piecing and assembling a quilt top and is working to master these skills. Someone who has the knowledge of how to sandwich, quilt and bind a quilt, but may not have necessarily accomplished the task yet.

- **Confident Beginner:** A quilter who has pieced and assembled several quilt tops and is comfortable with the process, and is now ready to move on to more challenging techniques and projects using at least two different techniques.

- **Intermediate:** A quilter who is comfortable with most quilting techniques and has a good understanding for design, color and the whole process. A quilter who is experienced in paper piecing, bias piecing and projects involving multiple techniques. Someone who is confident in making fabric selections other than those listed in the pattern.

- **Advanced:** A quilter who is looking for a challenging design. Someone who knows she or he can make any type of quilt. Someone who has the skills to read, comprehend and complete a pattern, and is willing to take on any technique. A quilter who is comfortable in her or his skills and has the ability to select fabric suited to the project. ●

Supplies

We would like to thank the following manufacturers who provided materials to our designers to make sample projects for this book.

Beach Glass, page 30: Sea from Space batik collection from Connecting Threads and "Sally by the Seashore" quilting design.

Charleston Twist, page 11: Fabrics from Hoffman California-International.

Flights of Fancy, page 6: Clover Meadow fabric collection from Moda Fabrics and Thermore batting from Hobbs.

I on U, page 22: Grunge by Basic Grey fabric collection from Moda Fabrics and Warm & White cotton batting from The Warm Company.

Spin Wheels, page 16: Stonehenge Gradations fabric collection from Northcott Fabric; Warm & Natural 100 percent cotton batting from The Warm Company and 50wt thread from Aurifil.

The Courtyard, page 36: Stiletto fabric collection from Moda Fabrics and Warm & Natural cotton batting from The Warm Company.

Twisted Fences, page 2: Jewel Box fabric collection from Island Batik and Soft & Bright batting from The Warm Company.

Special Thanks

Please join us in thanking the talented designers
whose work is featured in this collection.

Lyn Brown
Charleston Twist, page 11

Terri Butler of Mama Said Sew, LLC
I on U, page 22

Kerry Foster
Square Dance, page 40

Robin Koehler of Nestlings by Robin
Beach Glass, page 30

Cathey Laird of Cathey Marie Designs
Spin Wheels, page 16

Nancy Scott
Twisted Fences, page 2

Julie Weaver
Flights of Fancy, page 6
The Courtyard, page 36

Annie's® Published by Annie's, 306 East Parr Road, Berne, IN 46711. Printed in USA. Copyright © 2020 Annie's. All rights reserved. This publication may not be reproduced in part or in whole without written permission from the publisher.

RETAIL STORES: If you would like to carry this publication or any other Annie's publication, visit AnniesWSL.com.

Every effort has been made to ensure that the instructions in this publication are complete and accurate. We cannot, however, take responsibility for human error, typographical mistakes or variations in individual work. Please visit AnniesCustomerService.com to check for pattern updates.

ISBN: 978-1-64025-135-9
2 3 4 5 6 7 8 9